FRANCHISING IN BOTSWANA 2014

Legal and Business Considerations

KENDAL H. TYRE, JR., EXECUTIVE EDITOR
DIANA VILMENAY-HAMMOND, MANAGING EDITOR
COURTNEY L. LINDSAY, II, ASSISTANT EDITOR

LEXNOIR FOUNDATION

FIRST QUARTER 2014

LexNoir Foundation is the charitable, educational arm of LexNoir, an international network of lawyers connecting the African Diaspora.

This publication, *Franchising in Botswana 2014: Legal and Business Considerations*, contains excerpts from *Franchising in Africa 2014: Legal and Business Considerations*. Both works are published by LexNoir Foundation and reflect the points of view of the authors and editors as of the date of publication and do not necessarily represent the opinions, interpretations, or positions of the law firms or organizations with which they are affiliated, nor the opinions, interpretations or positions of LexNoir Foundation or LexNoir.

Nothing contained in this book is to be considered as the rendering of legal advice, either generally or in connection with any specific issues or case. Readers are responsible for obtaining advice from their own legal counsel or other professional. This book, any forms and agreements or other information herein are intended for educational and informational purposes only.

Table of Contents

Franchising in Botswana

Bonzo Makgalemele
Chibanda, Makgalemele & Company

Bibliography of International Franchise Resources

Kendal H. Tyre, Jr., Diana Vilmenay-Hammond, Pierce Haesung
Han, Courtney L. Lindsay, II, and Keri McWilliams
Nixon Peabody LLP

Acknowledgment

This book could not have been written without the hard work and dedication of each of the contributing authors and editors. Thank you.

We would like to acknowledge and extend our heartfelt gratitude to Michael Collier and Maria Stallings of the Washington, D.C. office of Nixon Peabody LLP for their invaluable assistance in revising, proofing, and editing this publication.

About the Editors and Authors

Kendal H. Tyre, Jr. – Kendal is a partner in the Washington, D.C. office of Nixon Peabody LLP. He handles domestic and cross-border transactions, including mergers and acquisitions, joint ventures, strategic alliances, licensing, and franchise matters.

In his franchise and licensing practice, Kendal counsels domestic and international franchisors, franchisees, licensors, licensees and distributors regarding U.S. state and federal franchise laws as well as foreign franchise legislation in a variety of jurisdictions. Kendal drafts and provides advice with regard to franchise and license agreements, disclosure documents and area development agreements and has extensive experience drafting and negotiating a variety of other commercial agreements. His client base spans the United States and foreign countries, including South Africa, Kenya, and the United Kingdom.

Kendal is a frequent contributor to franchise publications and a frequent speaker at franchise programs held by the American Bar Association Forum on Franchising and the International Franchise Association.

Kendal is co-chair of the firm's Diversity Action Committee and its Africa Group. Kendal is also the executive director of LexNoir Foundation.

E-mail address: ktyre@nixonpeabody.com

Diana Vilmenay-Hammond – Diana is an attorney in the Washington, D.C. office of Nixon Peabody LLP. She is a member of the firm's Franchise & Distribution Team.

In her franchise practice, Diana works with domestic and international franchisors on transactional and litigation matters. Specifically, she counsels franchisor clients regarding state and federal franchise laws, disclosure and registration obligations.

Diana drafts and negotiates various commercial agreements, including international franchise and development agreements.

Diana has co-authored numerous articles on franchising and frequently co-hosted the Nixon Peabody franchise law webinar series. Topics have included:

- "Franchise Case Law Round-Up: Implications for Your Franchise," February 15, 2012;
- "Social Media Part II: Best Practices in Protecting Your Brand in the New Media," September 14, 2010; and
- "The Awuah Case: Bellwether or Outlier," May 11, 2010

Diana received her J.D. from Howard University School of Law and her B.A. from Georgetown University. She is a member of the American Bar Association (Forum on Franchising).

Email address: dvilmenay@nixonpeabody.com

Pierce Haesung Han – Pierce is an associate in Nixon Peabody's Global Business & Transactions Group. Pierce focuses his practice on three main areas, assisting clients with a variety of complex business transactions.

- Mergers & Acquisitions: Providing assistance to both public and private clients with various mergers and acquisitions, performing due diligence, drafting and negotiating transaction documents, and facilitating closing and post-closing mechanics.
- International Commercial Transactions: Drafting and negotiating a variety of commercial agreements, including international franchise and development agreements, license agreements, and purchase and sale agreements.
- Federal Securities Law Matters: Assisting public and private clients regarding federal securities laws and stock exchange rules relating to corporate governance and disclosure.

Pierce serves as the Secretary of the Asian Pacific Bar Association Educational Fund (an affiliate of the Asian Pacific American Bar Association of the Greater Washington, D.C. Area).

Pierce received his J.D. from Georgetown University Law Center and his B.A. from Case Western Reserve University. He is admitted to practice in the State of New York and the District of Columbia.

E-mail address: phan@nixonpeabody.com

Courtney L. Lindsay II – Courtney is an associate in Nixon Peabody's Corporate and Finance practice. In his corporate practice, Courtney assists for-profit and non-profit entities with transactional matters and corporate governance. In various capacities, Courtney has been involved in multiple merger and acquisition transactions, including drafting and managing due diligence.

Previously, Courtney worked in the legal and business affairs department at a national cable network, where he handled matters related to the network's LLC agreement, including drafting board and member consent agreements.

Courtney received his J.D. from the University of Virginia School of Law and his B.A. from the University of Virginia. He is admitted to practice in the Commonwealth of Virginia and the District of Columbia.

E-mail address: clindsay@nixonpeabody.com

Keri McWilliams – Keri is an associate in the Franchise & Distribution team of Nixon Peabody LLP. Keri works with clients on a number of franchising issues, including obtaining and maintaining franchise registrations in various states, responding to state inquiries regarding trade practices, ongoing compliance with state and federal regulations, and updating franchise disclosure documents. She also handles franchise sales counseling and franchise system issues.

Keri is a member of the American Bar Association's Forum on Franchising, and the Federal and Minnesota State bar associations. She is also a member of Minnesota Women Lawyers and the Minnesota Association of Black Lawyers, and a volunteer in the Volunteer Lawyers Network.

Keri received her J.D. from the Georgetown University Law Center and her B.F.A. from Washington University. She is admitted to practice in the District of Columbia and Minnesota.

E-mail address: kmcwilliams@nixonpeabody.com

Bonzo Makgalemele – Bonzo is a senior partner at Chibanda, Makgalemele & Company in Gaborone, Botswana. She heads the Commercial Division of her firm. Her practice area consists mainly of corporate and commercial work including intellectual property, commercial agreements, commercial litigation, procurement, legislative reviews, policy formulation and privatization. She is admitted to practice in The Supreme Court of South Africa and The High Court of Botswana. Based in Gaborone and founded in 1994, her firm is a multi-practice law firm. Bonzo received her Bachelor of Laws degree from the University of Botswana in 1990, a post graduate certificate in Advanced Corporate and Securities Law from the University of South Africa in 2005, and a certificate in Infrastructure Project Finance from the Institute of Public Private Partnership in 2006.

E-mail address: BonzoM@cmclaw.co.bw

About the Book

Franchising in Botswana 2014: Legal and Business Considerations contains excerpts from the larger work, *Franchising in Africa 2014: Legal and Business Considerations*. Both books serve as practical, succinct, easy-to-use reference tools for lawyers, business people and academics to use in navigating the myriad laws and business issues impacting franchise arrangements on the African continent.

This book provides an overview of the franchise industry in Botswana and addresses the typical legal issues confronted when expanding a franchise system in Botswana. The larger work, *Franchising in Africa 2014: Legal and Business Considerations*, covers those laws governing franchising in fifteen other African countries – Angola, Burundi, Cape Verde, Democratic Republic of Congo, Egypt, Ethiopia, Ghana, Kenya, Mozambique, Nigeria, Rwanda, South Africa, Tunisia, Zambia and Zimbabwe.

In both books, an author, who is a legal expert in the designated jurisdiction, addresses the basic questions that a franchise lawyer would need to know to competently represent a client in expanding their franchise system to that country.

Each country chapter organizes a discussion of that country's laws under various headings and in a uniform format. Topics were sent to each country's author in the form of a questionnaire, and each author drafted responses to the questions presented. A general overview relating to the political and economic history of the country at the beginning of each chapter provides an initial context for the regulatory framework. [1]

---

[1] The source of information for these sections is the Central Intelligence Agency, https://www.cia.gov/library/publications/the-world-factbook/ (last visited November 3, 2013).

Apart from an overview of the legal framework for franchising, each book contains other articles and resources that should prove useful to those in the franchise industry.

The authors for each chapter are listed at the beginning of a chapter and their biographical information is listed in the previous section, *About the Editors and Authors*.

Readers should always consult with local counsel in the relevant jurisdiction instead of relying solely on the information contained in this book. The laws governing franchising are evolving and local counsel in Botswana are best positioned to provide timely, relevant advice applying the current law to the particular facts of a case.

Franchising in Botswana

Bonzo Makgalemele

Chibanda, Makgalemele & Company

Gaborone, Botswana

Botswana

I.   Introduction

A.   Historical Background of Country

Formerly the British protectorate of Bechuanaland, Botswana adopted its new name upon independence in 1966. Four decades of uninterrupted civilian leadership, progressive social policies, and significant capital investment have created one of the most dynamic economies in Africa. Mineral extraction, principally diamond mining, dominates economic activity, though tourism is a growing sector due to the country's conservation practices and extensive nature preserves.

B.   Economy of the Country

Botswana has maintained one of the world's highest economic growth rates since independence in 1966, though growth fell below 5% in 2007–08, and turned sharply negative in 2009, with industry falling nearly 30%. Although the economy recovered in 2010, growth has remained flat. Through fiscal discipline and sound management, Botswana transformed itself into a middle-income country with a per capita GDP of US13,100 in 2010. Two major investment services rank Botswana as the best credit risk in Africa. Diamond mining has fueled much of the expansion and currently accounts for more than one-third of GDP, 70–80% of export earnings, and about one-third of the government's revenues. Botswana's heavy reliance on a single luxury export was a critical factor in the sharp economic contraction of 2009. Tourism, financial services, subsistence farming, and cattle raising are other key sectors. Although unemployment was 17.8% in 2009 according to official reports, unofficial estimates place it as much as double the official estimate. The prevalence of HIV/AIDS that remains second highest in the world and an expected leveling off in diamond mining production within the next two decades overshadow long-term prospects. A major international diamond company signed a 10-year deal with Botswana in 2013 to move its rough stone sorting and trading division from London to Gaborone by

Botswana

the end of 2013. This move may support Botswana's downstream diamond industry.

C. Franchise Legal Overview

Under the Botswana law, there is no specific law that regulates franchise agreements and/or transactions. The franchise agreement is seen as a contractual agreement between the parties and thus contract law will govern such an agreement.

II. Regulatory Requirements

A. Pre-Sale Disclosure

Please describe any pre-sale franchise disclosure or similar requirements that may apply to franchise transactions.

No pre-sale franchise disclosure or similar requirements apply to franchise transactions under the laws of Botswana.

Botswana does not have specific legislation on franchising. In many instances, the contracting parties simply enter into a franchise agreement to set the terms and conditions that will govern their conduct with respect to the franchise. If any dispute arises the common law principles can be invoked by the courts to resolve matters.

B. Governmental Approvals, Registrations, Filing Requirements

Please describe any necessary government approvals, registrations, or filing requirements that may apply to franchise transactions.

Botswana law does not provide that the effectiveness of a franchise transaction is dependent on any formalities beyond the execution of a written contract, such as government approvals, registration or filing requirements.

Botswana

See, however, Section V (Trademarks) of this chapter relating to the registration of licenses with trademark authorities.

Under the Companies Act of Botswana, there is a requirement that every company and/or trade name to be used within the jurisdiction must be registered with the Registrar of Companies, Trademarks and Patents ("RGTP").

C.   Limits of Fees and Typical Term of Franchise Agreement

Please describe any limits upon the nature and extent of fees and the term of a typical franchise agreement.

There are no limits to fees. As stated, a franchise agreement is a contractual agreement between parties. They are free to agree on terms and conditions and to be bound by the terms to which they agree. However, the terms and conditions should fully comply with the principles of public policy.

III.   Currency

If all payments under a franchise agreement must be made in immediately available U.S. Dollars, please advise as to any restrictions, reporting requirements, or regulations concerning the exchange, repatriation, or remittance of U.S. Dollars.

There are no specific restrictions on payments made available in U.S. Dollars. It will depend on the parties' contractual agreement.

IV.   Taxes, Tariffs, and Duties

Please do not provide any in-depth comments on tax structuring. However, please provide your general comments on the typical amount of withholding tax that would apply and whether a "gross-up" provision contained in a franchise agreement would be enforceable in your country.

Botswana

The *Value Added Tax Act* (*Cap 50:03* of the Laws of Botswana), provides for a value added tax (VAT) on any activity that is carried on in Botswana (or partly therein) involving the supply of goods or services for consideration. Corporate income tax is levied on all Botswana-sourced taxable income of all companies other than tax exempt bodies.

A.   Applicable Rate

In Botswana, withholding tax is mainly a three (3) tier system.

1.   Dividends.

A withholding tax of 15% is levied on all dividends paid by a resident company to a resident or a non-resident.

2.   Interest.

A 15% withholding tax is levied on interest paid to non-residents and 10% on interest paid to residents. This tax may not be offset against corporate liability.

3.   Royalties.

The withholding tax on royalty payments made to non-residents is 15%. The withholding tax on royalties may not be offset against the corporate liability.

STATUTORY AND DOUBLE TAXATION AGREEMENT WITHHOLDING TAX RATES

	Construction contracts payments	Interest	Dividends	Commercial Royalties	Management or Consultancy Fees	Payments to Entertainers and Sports persons	Rent	Commission/ brokerage fees	Surplus mine rehabilitation funds
Statutory Rates									
Residents	3%	10%	7.5%	-	-	-	5%	10%	10%
Non-Residents	3%	15%	7.5%	15%	15%	10%	5%	10%	10%
Treaty Countries	**Treaty rates**								
Barbados	3%	10%	5%/12%	10%	10%	10%	5%	10%	-
France	3%	10%	5%/12%	10%	7.5%	10%	5%	7.5%	-
India	3%	10%	7.5%/10%	10%	10%	10%	5%	10%	-

Botswana

	Construction contracts payments	Interest	Dividends	Commercial Royalties	Management or Consultancy Fees	Payments to Entertainers and Sports persons	Rent	Commission/ brokerage fees	Surplus mine rehabilitation funds
Lesotho	3%	10%	10%/15%	10%	10%	10%	5%	10%	-
Mauritius	3%	12%	5%/10%	12.5%	15%	10%	5%	15%	-
Namibia	3%	10%	10%	10%	15%	10%	5%	15%	-
Russia	3%	10%	5%/10%	10%	10%	10%	5%	10%	-
Seychelles	3%	7.5%	5%/10%	10%	10%	10%	5%	10%	-
South Africa	3%	10%	10%/15%	10%	10%	10%	5%	10%	-
Swaziland	3%	10%	10%/15%	10%	10%	10%	5%	10%	-
Sweden	3%	7.5%	5%/10%	10%	15%	10%	5%	15%	-
UK	3%	10%	5%/12%	10%	7.5%	10%	5%	7.5%	-
Zimbabwe	3%	10%	5%/10%	10%	10%	10%	5%	10%	-

B.　Gross-up Clauses

Gross-up provisions may be permissible depending on the agreement made between the parties to a contractual agreement.

V.　Trademarks

Please advise us as to whether there are any special requirements for granting a valid trademark license, including the use of a registered user agreement or a short trademark license agreement and any required filing of such an agreement with the trademark authorities.

Intellectual property rights in Botswana are governed by the *Industrial Property Act Chapter 68:03*. Under *Section 67 of the Act*, owners of trademarks are entitled to enter into contracts to license the use of trademarks by others. Section 67 provides for effective control by the licensor of the quality of the goods or services under which such trademark is being licensed.

Section 71 of the same Act stipulates that a license contract concerning a registered trademark has to be filed and recorded by the Registrar in the appropriate register.

In Botswana, the registration of trademarks is regulated under the *Industrial Property Act, 2010*. Under *Section 76*, provision is

Botswana

made for registration of a trademark. This process involves the filing of a written application plus the prescribed fee. This fee can be revised by the Minister of Trade and Industry from time to time. For every application for registration of a trademark, *Article 4 of the Paris Convention* shall apply (right of priority).

After filing, the Registrar of Trademarks shall assess the application to verify that it meets the standard requirements under the Act.

Section 92 of the Act deals with licensing for the use of the trademark by the registered proprietor, to the effect that any license so issued shall provide for the effective control by the licensor of the quality of the goods or services of the license in connection with which the mark is used.

The regulatory authority reserves the right to reject registration of a trademark, if it fails to meet the specified standards of the definition of a "mark" under *Section 74(1)*.

Section 74(1) provides that a mark is not capable of registration if (i) it fails to distinguish the goods or services of one business from the other, (ii) is contrary to public policy or morality, (iii) is likely to mislead the public with regard to geographical origin or identical to a mark already in existence, (iv) the mark has acquired status of custom to be used in the particular trade, or (v) it is similar to what can be referred to as national emblems, flags or any official government mark.

VI.   Restrictions on Transfer

Please advise as to whether there are any restrictions (1) on a franchisor to restrict transfers by a master franchisee, any interest in a master franchisee, or the assets of the master franchisee or (2) the ability of a master franchisee to control and/or restrict transfers of a subfranchisee's rights under a master franchise agreement, interest in the subfranchisee, or the assets of the subfranchisee.

Botswana

A. In Relation to Master Franchisee

Under Botswana Law there is no specific regime governing the franchise agreement. The parties may agree on any provision that is not against the law or public policy.

1. Assignment

Generally, neither party may assign its contractual position without the prior consent of the other party. While it is common for franchise agreements to subject the franchisee's right to assign its contractual position to the consent of the franchisor, this also applies automatically per direct operation of the law, if the agreement does not expressly provide for such a rule.

2. Change of Control

It is permissible under Botswana law to subject to the franchisor's consent the right of the franchisee's shareholders to transfer their interest in the share capital of a franchisee.

3. Transfer of Assets

A clause by virtue of which the franchisee becomes obliged, upon termination of the franchise agreement, to transfer to the franchisor (or to another entity designated by the franchisor) all assets used in the franchise is permissible and also common in franchise agreements. The parties are free to determine whether such provision shall be included in the agreement and, if so, the mechanism to calculate the value of these assets.

B. In Relation to Subfranchisees.

1. Assignment

Neither party may assign its contractual position without the prior consent of the other. Therefore, although it may not be expressly provided for in the subfranchise agreement, a party may not assign its contractual position without the other's approval.

Moreover, the parties may also agree to subject the subfranchisee's right to assign its contractual position to the consent of the franchisor.

2. Change of Control

It is permissible under Botswana law to subject to the franchisor's consent the right of the franchisee's shareholders to transfer their interest in the share capital of a franchisee.

3. Transfer of Assets

The parties may agree on any terms as to how the assets may be transferred upon termination of the franchise. The parties are also at liberty to include any other clauses in the franchise agreement relating to transfer of such assets and how to value the assets upon such transfer.

VII. Termination

Please advise us as to any laws relating to termination in your country, such as agency laws, required indemnity provisions, notice or "good cause" requirements, or other laws affecting termination of a franchise agreement. Please describe.

A franchise agreement will terminate in the same manner as any other contract. Termination will arise upon the mutual agreement or by breach of performance of material contractual obligation by either of the parties. A franchise agreement may also be terminated due to unforeseen occurrence or other conditions.

Botswana

VIII. Governing Law, Jurisdiction, and Dispute Resolution

A.   Choice of Law of Foreign Jurisdiction

Please confirm whether the choice of law of a foreign jurisdiction would likely to be upheld under the law of the country, except for certain matters such as trademarks, bankruptcy, and competition matters, which we assume would be governed by the law in your country.

The choice of law designated by the parties will be upheld in Botswana as long as the parties agreed upon it. However, the choice of law should not be against the public policy of Botswana. If there is no choice of law assigned and chosen by the parties, the jurisdiction of Botswana law will take precedence.

B.   International Arbitration Dispute Resolution

Please confirm that a court in your country would honor an election of international arbitration dispute resolution, and therefore refuse to hear any disputes arising under a franchise agreement.

The law in Botswana regulating and governing arbitration is set out in the *Arbitration Act Chapter 06.01* of the *Botswana Laws*. Upon a dispute arising, parties are free to choose their arbitrators or mediators. They are also free to choose their seat of arbitration resolution.

The recognition and enforcement of *Foreign Arbitral Award Act, Chapter 06:02 of Botswana Laws* ("FAA") governs foreign arbitral awards made somewhere other than in Botswana. It also gives effect to some provisions of the *Convention on the Recognition and Enforcement of Foreign Arbitral Awards* (the "New York Convention"). Botswana is a signatory to the convention.

9

Botswana

Section 3(2) of the FAA provides that the provisions of the act shall apply to awards arising under legal relationships whether contractual or not as long as they are considered commercial relationships under the laws of Botswana.

Section 3(3) of the FAA provides that no arbitral award made in any country that is party to the New York Convention shall be enforceable in Botswana, unless similar awards made in Botswana would be enforceable in such country. Local courts can intervene or challenge the award only if the following has occurred:

- the subject matter of the dispute is not capable of settlement by arbitration under the law of that country;

- recognition of such award would be contrary to the public policy of that country;

- one of the parties was under some incapacity;

- the agreement is not valid under the law to which the parties have subjected it or under the law of the country where the award was made;

- the party against whom the award is invoked was not given proper notice of the appointment of the arbitrator or notice of arbitration proceedings to present his case;

- the award deals with a dispute not contemplated by or not falling within the terms of the submission;

- the composition of the arbitral authority is not in accordance with the agreement of the parties; and

- the award has not yet become binding on the parties, has been set aside or suspended by a competent authority of the country in which or under the law of which that award was made.

Finally, obtaining recognition of a foreign arbitral award under the laws of Botswana entails following the procedure set out in the New York Convention.

IX. Non-Competition Provisions

If the franchise agreement prohibits the master franchisee from engaging in certain competitive activities during the term of the agreement, and for a 12-month period after the termination or expiration of the agreement, please comment on the enforceability of non-competition covenants in your country.

Generally, since there is no specific legal regime governing franchise agreements, the parties themselves may agree on competition provisions. However, such provisions shall not be against public policy of Botswana law and should also not hinder others from engaging in and competing in the particular market.

X. Language Requirements

Does the law in your country require that a franchise agreement be translated into the local language in order to be enforceable between the parties?

The English language is predominantly used in commercial transactions. There is no requirement for an agreement to be translated into Setswana, the national language of Botswana.

XI. Other Significant Matters

Please advise as to whether there are any significant matters not addressed above of which a franchisor should be aware in connection with its entering into a franchise agreement in your country.

There are no other significant matters to be addressed.

Botswana

Bibliography of International Franchise Resources

Kendal H. Tyre, Jr., Diana Vilmenay-Hammond, Pierce Haesung Han, Courtney L. Lindsay, II, and Keri McWilliams

Nixon Peabody LLP

Washington, D.C.

I.   General International Resources

Mark Abell, Gary R. Duvall, and Andrea Oricchio Kirsh, *International Franchise Legislation* B1, ABA FORUM ON FRANCHISING (1996)

Kathleen C. Anderson and Anthony M. Stiegler, *Put Muscle in Your Marks: Enforcing Intellectual Property Rights* W14, ABA FORUM ON FRANCHISING (1995)

Richard M. Asbill and Jane W. LaFranchi, *International Franchise Sales Laws—A Survey* W7, ABA FORUM ON FRANCHISING (2005)

Jeffery A. Brimer, Alison C. McElroy, and John Pratt, *Going International: What Additional Restraints Will You Face?* W4, ABA FORUM ON FRANCHISING (2011)

Michael G. Brennan, Alexander Konigsberg, and Philip F. Zeidman, *Globetrotting: A Workshop on International Franchising* 10/W8, ABA FORUM ON FRANCHISING (1994)

Michael G. Brennan, Alexander Konigsberg, and Philip F. Zeidman, *Globetrotting: Strategies for Launching U.S. Franchisors Abroad* 2/P2, ABA FORUM ON FRANCHISING (1994)

Christopher P. Bussert and Jennifer Dolman, *Regaining Your Trademark After Abandonment or Misappropriation* W7, ABA FORUM ON FRANCHISING (2011)

Ronald T. Coleman and Linda K. Stevens, *Trade Secrets and Confidential Information: Rights and Remedies* W2, ABA FORUM ON FRANCHISING (2000)

Finola Cunningham, *Commerce Department Helps Franchisors Go Global*, in FRANCHISING WORLD 63 (Dec. 2005)

Michael R. Daigle and Alex S. Konigsberg, *Meeting Off-Shore Disclosure and Contract Requirements* F/W13, ABA FORUM ON FRANCHISING (1992)

Jennifer Dolman, Robert A. Lauer, and Lawrence M. Weinberg, *Structuring International Master Franchise Relationships for Success and Responding When Things Go Awry* W22, ABA FORUM ON FRANCHISING (2007)

Gary R. Duvall, Paul Jones, and Jane LaFranchi, *Planning for the International Enforcement of Franchise Agreements* W6, ABA FORUM ON FRANCHISING (1999)

William Edwards, *International Expansion: Do Opportunities Outweigh Challenges?* in FRANCHISING WORLD (February 2008)

George J. Eydt and Stuart Hershman, *Bringing a Foreign Franchise System to the United States* W9, ABA FORUM ON FRANCHISING (2009)

William A. Finkelstein and Louis T. Pirkey, *International Trademarks* W15, ABA FORUM ON FRANCHISING (1991)

William A. Finkelstein, *Protecting Trademarks Internationally: Current Strategies and Developments* B3, ABA FORUM ON FRANCHISING (1996)

Stephen Giles, Lou H. Jones, and Lawrence Weinberg, *Negotiating and Documenting Complex International Franchise Agreements* W21, ABA FORUM ON FRANCHISING (2006)

Steven M. Goldman, Stephen Giles, Marc Israel, and Stanley Wong, *Competition Round Up from Around the World* LB2, ABA FORUM ON FRANCHISING (2004)

David C. Gryce and E. Lynn Perry, *Trademarks and Copyrights in the International Arena* 6/W4, ABA FORUM ON FRANCHISING (1993)

Kenneth S. Kaplan, Andrew P. Loewinger, and Penelope J. Ward, *System Standards in International Franchising* W14, ABA FORUM ON FRANCHISING (2005)

Edward Levitt and Jorge Mondragon, *A Survey of International Legal Traps and How to Avoid Them—Beyond the Franchise Laws* W20, ABA FORUM ON FRANCHISING (2007)

Ned Levitt, Kendal H. Tyre, and Penny Ward, *The Impossible Dream: Controlling Your International Franchise System* W4, ABA FORUM ON FRANCHISING (2010)

Michael K. Lindsey and Andrew P. Loewinger, *International (Non-U.S.) Franchise Disclosure Requirements* W9, ABA FORUM ON FRANCHISING (2002)

Andrew P. Loewinger and John Pratt, *Recent Changes and Trends in International Franchise Laws* W4, ABA FORUM ON FRANCHISING (2008)

Andrew P. Loewinger and Thomas M. Pitegoff, *Avoiding the Long Arm of the Law in International Franchising: Issues and Approaches* W8, ABA FORUM ON FRANCHISING (1995)

Craig J. Madson and Katherine C. Spelman, *Similarity and Confusion in the Intellectual Property Arena* W11, ABA FORUM ON FRANCHISING (1997)

Christopher A. Nowak, John Pratt, and Carl E. Zwisler, *Franchising Internationally with Countries with Opaque Legal Systems* W20, ABA FORUM ON FRANCHISING (2006)

E. Lynn Perry and John L. Sullivan Jr., *Trademark Compliance and Enforcement Techniques* E/W12, ABA FORUM ON FRANCHISING (1992)

Marcel Portmann, *Franchising Sector Proves Global Reach*, in FRANCHISING WORLD (January 2007)

John Pratt and Luiz Henrique O. do Amaral, *Civil Law for Common Law Practitioners (or How to Draft an Agreement for Use Overseas)* W4, ABA FORUM ON FRANCHISING (2002)

Kirk W. Reilly, Robert F. Salkowski and Geoffrey B. Shaw, *Determining the Rules of Engagement in Litigation Here and Abroad* W5, ABA FORUM ON FRANCHISING (2008)

Catherine Riesterer and Frank Zaid, *Basics of International Franchising* L/B2, ABA FORUM ON FRANCHISING (1997)

W. Andrew Scott and Christopher N. Wormald, *Stranger in a Strange Land: Contrasting Franchising in International Expansion* W2, ABA FORUM ON FRANCHISING (2003)

Donald Smith and Erik Wulff, *International Franchising: The Unraveling of an International Franchise Relationship* 15/W13, ABA FORUM ON FRANCHISING (1993)

Frank Zaid, Pamela Mills, and Michael Santa Maria, *Essential Issues in International Franchising* LB/1, ABA FORUM ON FRANCHISING (2001)

II.   African Resources

Joyce G. Mazero and J. Perry Maisonneuve, *Franchising in the Middle East and North Africa* W2, ABA FORUM ON FRANCHISING (2009)

Kendal H. Tyre, Jr. and Diana Vilmenay-Hammond, *Franchise World: A Burgeoning Middle Class Spurs Franchise Investment in Africa*, MINORITY BUSINESS ENTREPRENEUR (November 2012)

Kendal H. Tyre, Jr., *IP Protection May Promote Additional Franchise Growth in Africa*, NIXON PEABODY LLP: FRANCHISING BUSINESS & LAW ALERT (September 2012)

Kendal H. Tyre, Jr., *Market Potential for Franchising in Africa*, NIXON PEABODY LLP: FRANCHISING BUSINESS & LAW ALERT (June 2011)

Kendal H. Tyre, Jr. and Courtney L. Lindsay, II, *Continued Growth of Franchising in Africa*, NIXON PEABODY LLP: FRANCHISE LAW ALERT (April 2013)

Kendal H. Tyre, Jr. and Courtney L. Lindsay, II, *Pan African Franchise Federation Holds Inaugural Meeting*, NIXON PEABODY LLP: AFRICA ALERT (June 2013)

Kendal H. Tyre, Jr. and Courtney L. Lindsay, II, *White House Encouraging Private Investment and Transparency in Sub-Saharan Africa*, NIXON PEABODY LLP: AFRICA ALERT (August 2012)

Kendal H. Tyre, Jr. and Diana Vilmenay-Hammond, *African Economic Growth Impacts Franchising on the Continent*, NIXON PEABODY LLP: FRANCHISE LAW ALERT (July 2012)

Kendal H. Tyre, Jr. and Diana Vilmenay-Hammond, *Franchising in Africa*, in FRANCHISING WORLD (August 2013)

John Sotos and Sam Hall, *African Franchising: Cross-Continent Momentum*, in FRANCHISING WORLD (June 2007)

A.   Angola

João Afonso Fialho, *Franchising in Angola*, in FRANCHISING IN AFRICA: LEGAL AND BUSINESS CONSIDERATIONS 91-105 (Kendal H. Tyre, Jr. & Diana Vilmenay-Hammond eds. 2012)

B.   Botswana

Bonzo Makgalemele, *Franchising in Botswana*, in FRANCHISING IN AFRICA: LEGAL AND BUSINESS CONSIDERATIONS 107-117 (Kendal H. Tyre, Jr. & Diana Vilmenay-Hammond eds. 2012)

C.   Cape Verde

João Afonso Fialho, *Franchising in Cape Verde*, in FRANCHISING IN AFRICA: LEGAL AND BUSINESS CONSIDERATIONS 119-132 (Kendal H. Tyre, Jr. & Diana Vilmenay-Hammond eds. 2012)

D.   Egypt

Girgis Abd El-Shahid, *Franchising in Eqypt*, in FRANCHISING IN AFRICA: LEGAL AND BUSINESS CONSIDERATIONS 133-142 (Kendal H. Tyre, Jr. & Diana Vilmenay-Hammond eds. 2012)

A. Safaa El Din El Oteifi, *Egypt*, in INTERNATIONAL FRANCHISING EGY/1 (Dennis Campbell gen. ed. 2011)

E.   Ethiopia

Yohannes Assefa and Biset Beyene Molla, *Franchising in Ethiopia*, in FRANCHISING IN AFRICA: LEGAL AND BUSINESS CONSIDERATIONS 143-157 (Kendal H. Tyre, Jr. & Diana Vilmenay-Hammond eds. 2012)

Kendal H. Tyre, Jr., Yohannes Assefa and Getachew Mengistie Alemu, *New Intellectual Property Regulation Requires Scramble to Protect Marks in Ethiopia*, NIXON PEABODY LLP: AFRICA ALERT (October 2013)

F.   Ghana

Divine K.D. Letsa and Hawa Tejansie Ajei, *Franchising in Ghana*, in FRANCHISING IN AFRICA: LEGAL AND BUSINESS CONSIDERATIONS 159-167 (Kendal H. Tyre, Jr. & Diana Vilmenay-Hammond eds. 2012)

G.   Libya

Kendal H. Tyre, Jr. & Diana Vilmenay-Hammond, *First U.S. Franchise Opens in Libya*, NIXON PEABODY LLP: AFRICA ALERT (August 2012)

H.   Mozambique

Diogo Xavier da Cunha, *Franchising in Mozambique*, in FRANCHISING IN AFRICA: LEGAL AND BUSINESS CONSIDERATIONS 169-182 (Kendal H. Tyre, Jr. & Diana Vilmenay-Hammond eds. 2012)

I.   Nigeria

Theo Emuwa and Bimbola Fowler-Ekar, *Franchising in Nigeria*, in FRANCHISING IN AFRICA: LEGAL AND BUSINESS CONSIDERATIONS 183-198 (Kendal H. Tyre, Jr. & Diana Vilmenay-Hammond eds. 2012)

Kendal H. Tyre, Jr. and Theo Emuwa, *Nigerian Franchising: Making Your Way Through the Thicket*, NIXON PEABODY LLP: FRANCHISE LAW ALERT (June 2005)

J.   South Africa

Eugene Honey, *Franchising and the New Consumer Protection Bill*, BOWMAN GILFILLAN (March 2008)

Eugene Honey, *Franchising and the Consumer Protection Bill*, BOWMAN GILFILLAN (May 2008)

Eugene Honey, *Pitfalls and Difficulties with the CPA*, ADAMS & ADAMS (March 2013)

Eugene Honey, *Disclosure is Compulsory*, ADAMS & ADAMS (May 2013)

Eugene Honey and Wim Alberts, *Fundamental Consumer Rights: The Right to Equality*, BOWMAN GILFILLAN (March 2009)

Eugene Honey and Wim Alberts, *The Reach of the Consumer Protection Bill: The Final*, BOWMAN GILFILLAN (March 2009)

Eugene Honey, *South Africa*, in GETTING THE DEAL THROUGH: FRANCHISE (2013) 172-178 (Philip F. Zeidman ed. 2013)

Taswell Papier, *Franchising in South Africa*, in FRANCHISING IN AFRICA: LEGAL AND BUSINESS CONSIDERATIONS 199-224 (Kendal H. Tyre, Jr. & Diana Vilmenay-Hammond eds. 2012)

Kendal H. Tyre, Jr., *A New Legal Landscape for Franchising in South Africa*, NIXON PEABODY LLP: FRANCHISING BUSINESS & LAW ALERT (September 2009)

K.   Tunisia

Yessine Ferah, *Franchising in Tunisia*, in FRANCHISING IN AFRICA: LEGAL AND BUSINESS CONSIDERATIONS 225-245 (Kendal H. Tyre, Jr. & Diana Vilmenay-Hammond eds. 2012)

Kendal H. Tyre, Jr., Diana Vilmenay-Hammond, and Yessine Ferah, *New Franchise Legislation in Tunisia*, NIXON PEABODY LLP: FRANCHISE LAW ALERT (September 2010)

L.   Zambia

Mabvuto Sakala, *Franchising in Zambia*, in FRANCHISING IN AFRICA: LEGAL AND BUSINESS CONSIDERATIONS 247-255 (Kendal H. Tyre, Jr. & Diana Vilmenay-Hammond eds. 2012)

14741752.1

www.ingramcontent.com/pod-product-compliance
Lightning Source LLC
Chambersburg PA
CBHW060325220326
41598CB00027B/4424